DATE DUE

WORLD BELIEFS AND CULTURES

Buddhism

Revised and Updated

Sue Penney

Heinemann Library
Chicago, Illinois

© 2001, 2008 Heinemann Library
Chicago, Illinois

Customer Service 888-454-2279
Visit our website at www.heinemannraintree.com

Designed by Steve Mead and Debbie Oatley
Printed and bound in the United States of America, North Mankato, MN.

13 12 11
10 9 8 7 6 5 4 3

New edition ISBNs: 1-4329-0312-8 (hardcover)
                     1-4329-0319-5 (paperback)
13-digit ISBNs: 978-1-4329-0312-1 (harcover)
                  978-1-4329-0319-0 (paperback)

The Library of Congress has cataloged the first edition as follows:
Penney, Sue.
    Buddhism / Sue Penney.
        p. cm. -- (World beliefs and cultures)
    Includes bibliographical references and index.
    ISBN 1-57572-354-9 (HC), 1-4034-4164-2 (Pbk.)
    1. Buddhism--Juvenile literature. [1. Buddhism.] I. Title. II. Series.

BQ4032 .P74   2000
294.3--dc21

022011   00-033478
006050R

Acknowledgments
The publishers would like to thank the following for permission to reproduce photographs: Alamy pp. **5** (Martin Jenkinson), **30** (World Religions Photo Library), **41** (Tibor Bognar); Andes Press Agency p. **38**; Ann and Bury Peerless pp. **13, 34**; Art Directors pp. **6** (Jane Sweeney), **22** (Fiona Good) Associated Press p. **27**; Circa Photo Library pp. **11, 15, 20, 25, 32, 39** (William Holtby), **23** (John Smith); Corbis p. **29**; Hutchison Library pp. **4, 7, 8, 10, 12, 18, 19, 24, 28** (Carlos Freire), **33** (Michael Macintyre) **40, 42**; Impact pp. **14, 26** (Mark Henley), **35** (Dominic Sansoni), **37**; Robin Bath pp. **17, 21, 31, 36, 43**. Background image on cover and inside book from istockphoto.com/Bart Broek.

Cover photo of the temple of Wat May in Laos reproduced with permission of © Masterfile/ R. Ian Lloyd.

The publishers would like to thank Mark A. Berkson for his comments in the preparation of this book.

Every effort has been made to contact copyright holders of any material reproduced in this book. Any omissions will be rectified in subsequent printings if notice is given to the publishers.

Contents

Some words are shown in bold, **like this**. You can find out what they mean by looking in the glossary.

Dates: In this book, dates are followed by the letters BCE (Before the Common Era) or CE (Common Era). This is instead of using BC (Before Christ) and AD (*Anno Domini*, meaning "in the year of our Lord"). The date numbers are the same in both systems.

Introducing Buddhism

The teachings we call Buddhism began in India about 2,500 years ago. The teacher was a man named Siddhartha Gautama, whom his followers call **Buddha**. "Buddha" is a special title that means "Enlightened One" or "Awakened One." **Enlightenment** is a special understanding—realizing the truth about the way things are. Buddhists believe that there were other Buddhas before Gautama, and there will be others in the future, but he is the one whose teachings are for the present age.

What do Buddhists believe?

Buddhists believe that everything in the world is impermanent, meaning that nothing lasts. They believe that when Buddha gained Enlightenment, he found the answer to why people suffer and the path to liberate people from suffering. They believe that if people follow the teachings of Buddha, then they, too, can gain Enlightenment. This means that many Buddhists believe everyone could become a Buddha. Buddhists do not believe in an all-powerful God. Their teachings have no need of such a being. They do not believe that Buddha himself was anything more than a human being. He is important because he achieved Enlightenment and chose to teach others the way to achieve it, too.

Nirvana

Buddhists believe in a continual cycle of birth, old age, illness, death, and "re-becoming," or **rebirth**. They do not believe in **reincarnation** (a soul being reborn in a different body), because they do not believe in a soul. This cycle of life is described in the word "**samsara**." Buddhists believe that the only escape is to gain Enlightenment. This will allow them to achieve **nirvana**, which is the end of suffering. They say that nirvana is the "blowing out of the fires" of greed, hatred, and ignorance, followed by a state of perfect peace and happiness. Buddhists believe that, ultimately, there are no words that can describe nirvana.

The lotus flower is used by Buddhists as a symbol because it rises out of the mud to become a beautiful flower.

Meditation

Buddhists try to reach nirvana by following Buddha's teachings. These include **meditation**, often called "mindfulness meditation." During meditation they aim to control their minds so that they can go "beyond" thought. This means training the mind to be aware of all things that arise—for example, thoughts or bodily sensations—without clinging to them or suppressing them. Going "beyond" thought means leaving behind worries about the world and rising above them. Buddhists believe that by meditating, they will become better people and will be able to achieve Enlightenment.

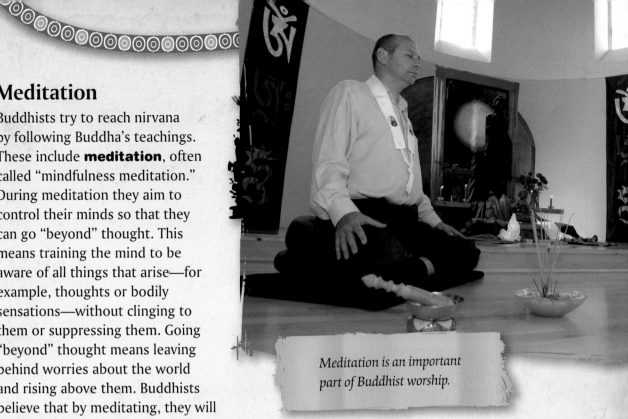

Meditation is an important part of Buddhist worship.

Buddhism is a system of thought, or **philosophy**, but we often use religious words to describe some of its practices. For example, in this book "worship" means the way Buddhists practice their beliefs, but it does not suggest that Buddhists are looking for God.

Buddhism fact check

◆ The teaching we call Buddhism began in India about 500 BCE.

◆ Buddhists follow the teachings of Siddhartha Gautama, called Buddha.

◆ Buddhists worship in **temples** and at home.

◆ The major teachings of Buddhism were compiled in a set of texts called the **Tripitaka**, which means "three baskets." These include teachings of Buddha (called **sutras**), rules regulating the lives of **monks** and **nuns** (called Vinaya), and philosophical texts (called Abhidharma).

◆ The symbol used for Buddhism is a wheel with eight spokes. The wheel is a reminder of the cycle of samsara, and the eight spokes are a reminder that one of Buddha's most important teachings was divided into eight parts. Another symbol is the lotus flower. This grows in mud, but rises to the top of the pond as a beautiful flower. Buddhists say it is a symbol of rising above everything imperfect in this life.

◆ No one is sure exactly how many Buddhists there are in the world. The official estimate is 375 million Buddhists worldwide, with about 1.5 million Buddhists in the United States.

The Life of Buddha

Siddhartha Gautama was an Indian prince. He was born in Lumbini, in what is today called Nepal, in the 5th century BCE.

The stories say that when Gautama was born, a wise man said that if he ever saw suffering, he would become a great religious leader rather than a great ruler. Gautama's father wanted an heir to succeed him, so he ordered that no one who was sick or old should be allowed near the prince. Gautama himself was not allowed to leave the palace grounds. Gautama grew up to be handsome and smart. He married a beautiful girl, and they had a son. He was rich and powerful—it seemed that his life had everything.

Many Buddhists come to visit the bo tree at Bodh Gaya.

However, Gautama became bored with his sheltered life, and one day he went riding outside the palace grounds. While he was out, he saw an old man, a sick man, and a funeral, with relatives weeping around the body. These things disturbed him very much. Then, he saw a holy man who was content and happy. He said he had given up his home and his family and wandered from place to place searching for the answers to the problem of suffering in the world.

Gautama was so troubled by what he had seen that he decided he, too, must try to find the answer to this problem. On the night before his 29th birthday, he left the palace. He changed his royal robes for the simple clothes worn by holy men and shaved his head.

The bo tree

The bo tree is a sort of fig tree. In 250 BCE a cutting from the tree at Bodh Gaya was taken to Sri Lanka, when Buddhism was introduced there, and planted. This tree is still alive and is believed to be the oldest tree in the world. The original tree at Bodh Gaya died in the 12th century CE, but in 1884 a cutting from the tree in Sri Lanka was taken back there. The tree grew, and Buddhists today can sit under it to meditate.

Gautama's search for Enlightenment

You can find the places mentioned in this book on the map on page 44.

For the next six years, Gautama traveled around India, spending time with teachers and monks. For several years he lived with five holy men, eating and drinking almost nothing. But he found that starving himself did not help him to find any answers, so he began eating and drinking again. He wanted to find the "**Middle Way**" between the indulgence of his life in the palace and severe self-denial. Gautama traveled on until at last he came to a great tree. Today, this is called the **bo tree**, which means "tree of wisdom," and the place is called Bodh Gaya. He sat under the tree and meditated.

Buddhists believe that during this time, Gautama was attacked by the evil spirit Mara, who sent demons to scare him and tried to tempt him away from his meditation. The attack had no effect. At last—according to the stories, on the night of the full moon, his 35th birthday—Gautama gained Enlightenment. In other words, he achieved insight into the way things are and freedom from suffering. Buddhists say this is a feeling of total peace, when you can stop thinking about yourself and become totally free.

From this time on, Siddhartha Gautama was called Buddha. According to Buddhist teaching, having achieved Enlightenment, Gautama could have left Earth, but he chose not to. He believed his knowledge should be passed on to others, so he spent the rest of his life teaching people about the right ways to live. He passed away (Buddhists do not say he died) at the age of 80. His body was **cremated**, and the ashes were placed in special burial mounds called **stupas**. Buddhists say that Buddha's passing away was when he entered **Parinirvana**. This is the name given to the "complete" nirvana after a Buddha's body has stopped living.

This "reclining Buddha" statue in Sri Lanka shows Buddha just before he entered Parinirvana.

The History of Buddhism

Buddhists believe that there were Buddhas before Siddhartha Gautama and there will be other Buddhas in the future. Therefore, they refer to Gautama's teaching as "the present Buddhist teaching." This began in India, when Gautama reached Enlightenment, because he chose to stay in the world to show others the best way to live.

First followers

Buddha's first followers were the five holy men with whom he had spent years when he was searching for Enlightenment. Before long, other people became interested in his teachings, too, and asked to join him. The group became known as the **sangha**. Buddha's first followers included his own son, Rahula. At first, women were not allowed, but Gautama was persuaded by his stepmother and his cousin to eventually agree that women, too, could join the group. For 45 years, Buddha spent his time traveling around India and neighboring countries, preaching and teaching.

This pillar was erected by Emperor Ashoka in Delhi, the capital of India, and is made of iron.

Emperor Ashoka

After Buddha had passed away, his followers carried on his teaching, and Buddhism continued to grow. The teaching about respecting all life caught the attention of Emperor Ashoka. He ruled almost the whole of India from 273 BCE to 232 BCE. He had been a hunter and soldier, but he became unhappy about the suffering and death he had caused. One day he met a group of Buddhist monks. He listened to their teachings and became a Buddhist himself. From then on, he tried to rule according to Buddhist teachings. He encouraged other people to become Buddhists and sent monks and nuns traveling from place to place, teaching about Buddhism.

The spread of Buddhism

From India, Buddhism spread to other countries, particularly because of Ashoka. His own son and daughter took Buddhism to Sri Lanka. By the 1st century CE, it had reached Nepal, Tibet, and China, where it grew slowly alongside Chinese religions. By the 9th century it was well established in China.

It also spread to China's neighboring countries. It reached Korea in the 4th century. In Myanmar (formerly Burma), it was important by the 5th century, and its spread was later helped by the Buddhist ruler Anawrahta. From there it spread to Thailand, Cambodia, Malaysia, and Laos. By the 8th century, it was well established in Japan.

Buddhism did not reach Western countries for hundreds of years. In the 19th century it traveled from Japan to the Americas, especially the west coasts. The first Buddhist **missionary** in England landed in 1893. In the same year, Buddhism was introduced at the World's Parliament of Religions, part of the Columbian Exposition held in Chicago.

As Buddhism spread to different countries, people who became Buddhists did not leave behind everything they had known before. The different groups began to emphasize different teachings. Within a short time, Buddhists had divided into three main schools: **Theravada**, **Mahayana**, and **Vajrayana** (sometimes called Mantrayana). Later, other smaller groups emerged—for example, **Zen** Buddhists. These groups have much in common, but also differ in important ways. Buddhist customs and particularly festivals are celebrated in quite different ways in different countries.

Mongolia
South Korea
Japan
China
Tibet
Nepal
Bhutan
Laos
India
Vietnam
Taiwan
Myanmar (Burma)
Thailand
Cambodia
Sri Lanka
Malaysia
Indonesia

Countries where Buddhism is a main religion

Countries where there are many Buddhists, though it is not a main religion

This map shows the countries where Buddhism is most important today.

Emperor Ashoka's columns

Ashoka ordered that pillars should be put up that marked where important things had happened to Buddha, with writing on them explaining what they were. He suggested that people should go on **pilgrimages** to these places. Ashoka also had his policies for government written up in the same way. Many of these writings still survive today. They show that Ashoka was a conscientious ruler who took Buddha's teachings about caring for others very seriously. For example, one of the tablets, called the Rock Edicts, reads, "Beloved of the Gods [for example, Ashoka] speaks thus: Father and mother should be respected and so should elders. Kindness to living beings should be made strong and the truth should be spoken. In these ways the **dharma** [Buddha's teaching] should be promoted. Likewise a teacher should be honored by his pupil, and proper manners should be shown toward relatives. This is an ancient rule that conduces to long life. Thus one should act. Written by the scribe Chapala."

The Main Schools of Buddhism

You can find the places mentioned in this book on the map on page 44.

All Buddhists follow the teachings of Buddha, but different groups do not follow them in exactly the same way. As Buddhism spread, it was influenced by religions that already existed in the countries to which it went. So, the ways in which Buddhism was practiced became different. In Buddhism the main groups are known as schools. There are three main schools: Theravada Buddhism, Mahayana Buddhism, and Vajrayana Buddhism. All of these schools have smaller groups.

A typical Theravada **Buddharupa** (statue of Buddha) is serene and calm.

Theravada Buddhism

"Theravada" means "Way of the Elders." Elders are respected leaders of a religion. Theravada Buddhist teachings are written in the language called **Pali**. Today, these are mainly read by monks. Theravada Buddhism is found mostly in Sri Lanka, Myanmar, Cambodia, Thailand, and Laos.

Theravada Buddhists emphasize the idea that each person must gain Enlightenment for him or herself. No one can do it for someone else. They believe that Buddha taught people how they should live, but he was only a man. The only way he can help people to gain Enlightenment today is through his teachings. Theravada Buddhists do not pray to Buddha.

Theravada Buddhists think that the best way to live is as a monk. A monk can concentrate on his religion because he has no responsibilities or possessions. In many places, some women become nuns and live in the same way as monks, although they do not follow exactly the same rules. Because of the importance that they attach to monks and nuns, Theravada Buddhists believe that it is an important part of their religious duty to give food and other gifts to the monks and **monasteries**.

Mahayana Buddhism

Mahayana Buddhism began in India in about 100 BCE. It is now more popular in China, Japan, Korea, and Tibet, and among Buddhists in some Western countries.

Mahayana Buddhism follows the same ideas as Theravada Buddhism, but in some cases it has changed the way they are understood and explained. "Mahayana" means "great vehicle." This is a way of saying that there is room for different ways to nirvana.

Belief in **bodhisattvas** is an important difference between Theravada and Mahayana Buddhists. A bodhisattva is a person who is destined to reach Enlightenment, but has postponed achieving it in order to stay in the world to help others achieve Enlightenment.

Both Theravada and Mahayana Buddhists use **rupas** of Buddha to help them in their worship. As a general rule, Theravada rupas show a Buddha who is calm, serious, and serene. Some Mahayana Buddhist rupas are jolly and smiling.

Vajrayana Buddhism

"Vajrayana" means "diamond vehicle" or "thunderbolt vehicle." Most followers of Vajrayana Buddhism are in Tibet, Mongolia, and Japan. Vajrayana Buddhism is similar to Mahayana Buddhism. However, it emphasizes a close relationship between a spiritual leader, sometimes called a guru, and a small group of disciples, or followers. The disciples spend a lot of time reciting phrases called **mantras**, performing sacred dances and gestures, and meditating. The followers keep many of their beliefs and practices secret from outsiders.

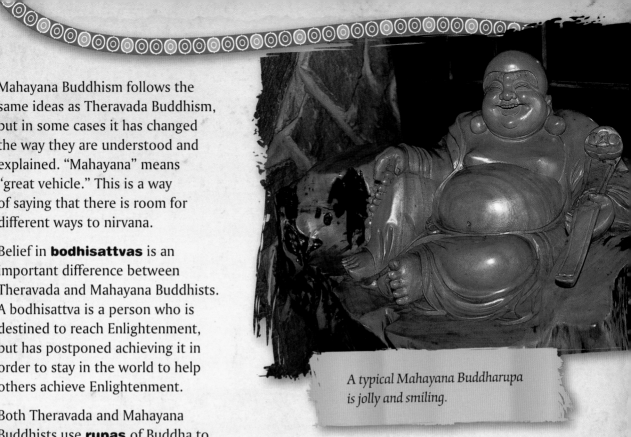

A typical Mahayana Buddharupa is jolly and smiling.

The Three Jewels

All Buddhists believe that the most important statements of Buddhist belief can be summed up in the Three Jewels. They were given this name because Buddhists believe that they are the most precious part of their belief.

I take refuge in Buddha [The Enlightened One]
I take refuge in the dharma [teaching]
I take refuge in the sangha [the Buddhist community]

A refuge is somewhere that is safe, so when Buddhists say that they take refuge, they are showing that these things are something that they can put at the center of their lives.

Schools of Mahayana Buddhism

There are many different schools in Mahayana Buddhism. Each one has its own particular beliefs and ways of practicing. As a general rule, Mahayana Buddhists are less likely to become monks and nuns. They believe that lay people (non-monks and nuns) are equally important.

Zen Buddhist monks spend many hours each day meditating. Here, a monk sits before the master (roshi).

Zen Buddhism

"Zen" is a Japanese word that means "meditation." Zen Buddhism is most popular in Japan, Korea (where it is called Seon), and China (where it is called Chan). Like all Buddhists, followers of Zen Buddhism aim to reach Enlightenment. Zen Buddhists say that you cannot reach Enlightenment by thinking about it—you have to go beyond your mind to achieve it. Zen Buddhists believe that all people have a "Buddha Nature," and that through meditation, they can realize this nature.

Zen Buddhists have their own ways of trying to reach Enlightenment, and they say that it comes as a flash of higher understanding. The majority of their time is spent in *zazen*—that is, sitting in meditation. Another approach to Zen meditation uses koans, which are paradoxical riddles and stories. The idea is to shock the mind out of its usual ways of thought.

Pure Land Buddhism

Pure Land (Jodo Shin Shu) Buddhism is particularly popular in Japan. It also has many followers in the United States. It teaches that this period in the world is so wicked that people cannot achieve nirvana on their own. The only hope is to pray to Buddha Amida, Lord of the Pure Land. The Pure Land is **Sukhavati**, understood by some to be a paradise full of fruits and flowers and by others to be a state of mind. Pure Land Buddhists teach that this is a stage on the way to nirvana, but it is a very different idea from the Theravada teaching about nirvana as an extinguishing of all the desires of life. A mantra used by followers of this school is called the Nembutsu, "Namu Amida Butsu," which means, "Praise the Amida Buddha."

Tibetan Buddhism

Tibetan Buddhists have their own **shrines** and way of worship. They hold the greatest respect for their leader, the **Dalai Lama**. They believe he is an appearance of the Bodhisattva Avalokiteshvara, who is most important for Tibetans. There is a mantra that is like a prayer to this bodhisattva. It is "Om mani padme hum." In English this means, "The jewel is in the lotus," but its true meaning cannot really be translated. The prayer is written on prayer wheels and prayer flags.

Prayer wheels are cylinders, usually made of bronze, with a prayer written on special paper rolled up in the center. They can be small enough to hold, but many temples have huge prayer wheels. The larger the wheel, the more powerful the prayer. As the wheels are turned and the flags blow in the wind, Tibetan Buddhists believe the prayer is repeated over and over. The prayers build up **merit**, the reward for doing good things.

Mudras (hand gestures), chants (a kind of singing), **mandalas** (special patterns), and mantras are important for Tibetan Buddhists. They believe they can help a person on his or her way to nirvana.

In 1959 the Chinese took over Tibet. They did not approve of Buddhist practices, and many monasteries and Buddhist monuments were destroyed. Thousands of Tibetans were killed in demonstrations. The Dalai Lama now lives in exile in Dharamsala, in northern India.

This prayer wheel is in a Tibetan Buddhist monastery.

A Zen story

There is a Zen Buddhist story about a young trainee in a monastery. He sat for a whole day in the **lotus position**. At last, the master appeared and asked him what he was doing. He said that he was trying to become a Buddha. The master picked up a stone and began to polish it. Curious, the young man asked what he was doing. "Making a mirror," replied the master. The trainee said, "But you can't make a mirror out of a stone." "Neither can any amount of sitting cross-legged make you a Buddha," said the master.

What Buddha Taught

You can find the places mentioned in this book on the map on page 44.

Most Buddhists agree that Buddha's teaching can be summed up in three parts. The first is the Three Marks of Existence, the second is the Four Noble Truths, and the third is the Noble Eightfold Path. Buddhists believe that, taken together, these three teachings show the best ways to live.

The Three Marks of Existence

The three marks of existence can be summed up in three words—**duhkha**, **anitya**, and **anatman**. "Duhkha" is often translated as "suffering," but it means more than that. "Duhkha" means "unsatisfactoriness," in the sense that the way that we normally live life produces discontent and suffering. "Duhkha" characterizes the way we experience the world when we are unenlightened. "Anitya" means "impermanence"—nothing lasts. Even "solid" things like mountains are always changing. Buddhists believe that nirvana is the escape from the suffering brought about by clinging to illusions of permanence. "Anatman" means "no soul." Buddha said that there is no such thing as a soul or a spirit. Each person has a body, thoughts, feelings, ideas, and awareness. These five parts, and the way they come together, make up each person. When a body dies, the parts fall apart and are re-assembled in a different way to make another person. What continues from one life to the next is **karma** (the "life force"), which a person creates while he or she is alive. The force of a good life will lead to a "higher" life next time. The force of a bad life will lead to a "lower" life next time.

Buddhists believe that everything in life is duhkha—unsatisfactory—but everyone should work to the best of their ability.

What Buddha said

The best of paths is the path of eight; the best of truths the four sayings. The best of states, freedom from passions. The best of men, the one who sees. This is the path, there is no other that leads to the purification of insight. Whoever goes on this path travels to the end of sorrow. (**Dhammapada** 20:273–6)

The Four Noble Truths

In his first sermon after he had achieved Enlightenment, Buddha preached to the five holy men with whom he had spent several years searching for the meaning of life. This took place at Sarnath, the Deer Park in Varanasi. Buddhists generally agree that the most important part of this sermon was the teaching called the Four Noble Truths. They are based around duhkha.

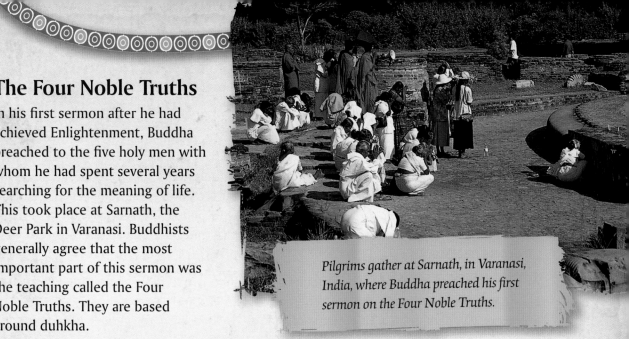

Pilgrims gather at Sarnath, in Varanasi, India, where Buddha preached his first sermon on the Four Noble Truths.

◆ *Life is duhkha.*
When we are unenlightened, the way we live produces discontent and suffering. The only release from duhkha is to achieve nirvana.
◆ *Duhkha is caused by attachment.*
We are forever "clinging" to things, each other, and ourselves in a mistaken effort at permanence.

◆ *Attachment can be overcome.*
Breaking out of the rebirth cycle can be achieved by gaining nirvana, which is freedom from all desires.
◆ *The way to overcome this cycle is the Noble Eightfold Path.*

The Noble Eightfold Path

The Noble Eightfold Path shows the Middle Way between extremes, which Buddhists should follow in their lives. "Right" means "best possible"—that is, using Buddhist teachings. All of these things need to be acted on together.

◆ *Right view*
Understanding the Four Noble Truths.
◆ *Right thought*
Using your mind in the right way so that you become unselfish.
◆ *Right speech*
Being kind and helpful when you speak, and not telling lies, swearing, or gossiping.
◆ *Right action*
Avoiding killing, stealing, or being dishonest. Being faithful to your husband or wife, not drinking alcohol or taking non-medicinal drugs.

◆ *Right livelihood*
Working to the best of your ability. The job you do should be useful and not involve anything that harms others.
◆ *Right effort*
Avoiding bad things and working hard to do good.
◆ *Right mindfulness*
Focusing your attention on your body, feelings, and consciousness to overcome bad things.
◆ *Right concentration*
Meditating in such a way as to have a true understanding of impermanence.

The Holy Books

At first, none of Buddha's teachings were written down. At the time when he was alive, not many people could read and write, so they were far more used to remembering things. However, soon after Buddha had passed away, people began to think that it would be a good idea to make sure there was a clear record of what he had said. All his followers knew the most important teachings, but few people knew everything that he had taught. Since his teachings were thought to be so important, a written record of all of them was necessary.

A special meeting of 500 Buddhist monks was arranged. All Buddha's teaching was recited by the **Venerable** Ananda and the Venerable Upali, who were two of Buddha's closest followers. ("Venerable" is a title that is often used by Buddhists for monks. It means someone who is very respected.) All the monks repeated the teaching together. This made sure that everyone agreed. This teaching was passed down by the monks. It was not written down for about 400 years, but in that time there were several meetings to check that it was still accurate and organize it.

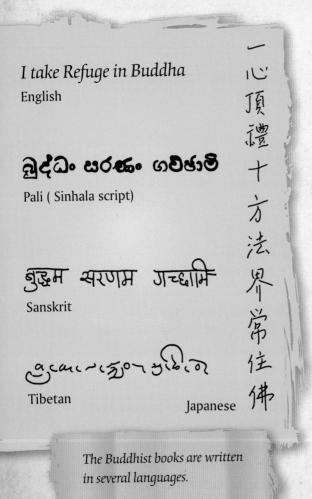

I take Refuge in Buddha
English

බුද්ධං පරණං ගච්ඡාමි
Pali (Sinhala script)

बुद्धम् सरणम् गच्छामि
Sanskrit

Tibetan

Japanese

The Buddhist books are written in several languages.

The two canons

The two most important collections of Buddha's teaching are called the Pali **Canon** and the **Sanskrit** canon. A canon is a collection of writings. It comes from the Greek word for a ruler used for measuring and is the word used in most religions to describe the holy books that are accepted as genuine. Pali and Sanskrit are the ancient languages in which the collections of teaching were made. The Pali canon was written down first. It is also called the Tripitaka, meaning "three baskets." It was probably given this name because the teachings were first written down on palm leaves, which were kept in baskets. In the days before paper was common, it was common for leaves to be used instead. The leaf was flattened, and then the words were etched (carved) into the leaves with a metal stylus. A stylus is like a pen with a sharp point that is used to scratch patterns. The leaf was then rubbed over with carbon ink, so that the pattern of the etching was filled and the letters showed up. The first two baskets of the Tripitaka contain the most important teachings for all Buddhists. Theravada and Mahayana Buddhists have different ideas about what should be included in the third basket.

Mahayana Buddhist books

In addition to Buddha's teachings, which all Buddhists accept, Mahayana Buddhists also have teachings that are particularly important to different groups. One of the most important texts for Mahayana Buddhists is the **Lotus Sutra**. There are also many documents in languages other than Sanskrit and Pali that form part of the teachings of different schools of Mahayana Buddhists. For Tibetan Buddhism, the Ka-guyur text is one of its most important collections of teaching. This has 108 volumes of teaching and 225 more volumes that explain the teachings.

In China there are thought to be 1,662 different teachings, and the **Diamond Sutra,** which dates from the 4th century CE, is among the most important. Many of the teachings were engraved on polished stone and rocks and can still be seen today. Some were written on dark blue paper, using gold or silver ink. In about the 8th century CE, Chinese Buddhists had the idea of carving mirror images of Chinese characters onto wooden blocks so that they could be used to print several copies of the sutras. This was how wood-block printing started. A copy of the Diamond Sutra, printed by this method in 868 CE, still exists today.

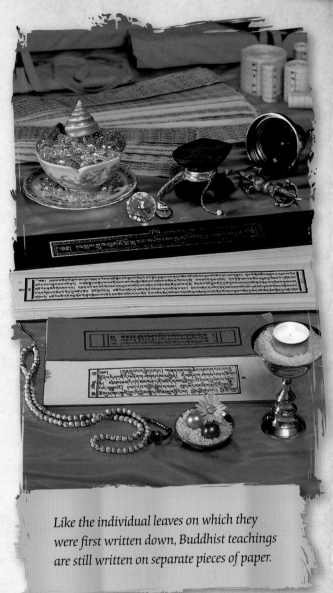

Like the individual leaves on which they were first written down, Buddhist teachings are still written on separate pieces of paper.

The two canons

From a very early stage, Buddhist Scriptures were written in two languages. This is the reason why many important Buddhist words can be spelled two ways. For example, the state that Buddhists are trying to achieve can be called nirvana or nibbana. "Nirvana" is the Sanskrit form and "nibbana" is the Pali form of the word. "Sutta" is the Pali form of the word for a small piece of teaching and "sutra" is the Sanskrit form. Neither form is "better" or "more correct" than the other. In this book, the Sanskrit form is the one that is used more often.

What the holy books say

The most important Buddhist teachings are the Tripitaka—the three baskets. Almost all Buddhists agree on the contents of the first two baskets, but Mahayana Buddhists have their own teachings in the third basket that are different from the teachings that Theravada Buddhists include.

Young Buddhist monks read the Scriptures at a monastery in India.

The Tripitaka

The first "basket" of the Tripitaka is called the Vinaya Pitaka, which means "discipline." It contains the rules for monks to follow, with some stories and other teachings. The second "basket" is the Sutra Pitaka, which contains most of the dharma—the teachings of Buddha. The third "basket" is the Abhidharma Pitaka, which means "higher teaching." Most of this basket consists of writings that explain Buddha's teachings.

The most important of these three baskets is the Sutra Pitaka, because it contains the teachings of Buddha. A sutra is a small piece of teaching. A well-known part of this basket is called the Dhammapada, which contains the most memorable sayings of Buddha. Buddhists spend a lot of time studying these words. The most important part is the section called the Path of Teaching, because this contains the Four Noble Truths and the Noble Eightfold Path. The Sutra Pitaka also contains stories about Buddha, including stories about his previous lives before he was Gautama.

Quotations from the holy books

The reason why Buddhists believe that the holy books are so important can be seen in these quotes from Buddha:

If you really want to see me, look at my teaching.
(Samyutta Nikaya)

Just before he passed away, Buddha said to his companion the Venerable Ananda:
When I am gone, do not say that you have no teacher. Whatever I have taught, let that be your teacher when I am gone.
(Mahaparinibbana Sutra—a Pali teaching)

Much of Buddha's teaching was about the importance of behaving in the right way. The first quotation below is from the Sanskrit Sutra of the 42 Chapters. This is believed to have been the first sutra to be translated into Chinese, when it was organized so that the teaching was in 42 sections.

Buddha said,
For human beings, ten things are evil. Three are of the body; four are of the mouth; and the other three are of the mind. The three evils of the body are needless killing, stealing, and sensual misconduct. The four evils of the mouth are saying one thing but meaning another, slander, lying, and improper language. The three evils of the mind are greed, anger, and foolishness.

Who is tactful and energetic,
And gains wealth by his own effort,
He will acquire fame by truth,
And friendship by giving.
He who has faith and is also truthful,
Virtuous, firm, and fond of giving;
By virtue of these four conditions
Will never in the hereafter feel sorry.
Truth and Restraint, Charity and Forbearance,
Are the greatest reformers of human beings.
(Alavaka Sutra)

People worship at the feet of a Buddharupa in Thailand.

Hold not a sin of little worth, thinking "this is little to me." The falling of drops of water will in time fill a jar of water. Even so the foolish man becomes full of evil, although he gather it little by little. Hold not a deed of little worth, thinking "this is little to me." The falling of drops of water will in time fill a jar. Even so, the wise man becomes full of good, although he gather it little by little.
(Dhammapada 9:121–2)

Symbols in Buddhism

The teachings of Buddhism include many ideas that are difficult to explain. Using symbols helps to make things clear. It also means that ideas can be explained without using words, which is useful when teachings are being translated into another language. The lotus flower, for example, is often used as a symbol for Buddhism. Flowers are often used as offerings at Buddhist shrines. They help to make the shrine attractive and they smell pleasant. However, they soon decay and die, which makes them a symbol of the belief that nothing lasts.

Buddha

There are thousands of Buddharupas (images of Buddha) in countries all over the world. They use many symbols. Buddha is usually shown in one of three positions—standing, sitting, or lying down. His hands are in different positions, showing an aspect of his teaching. If he is standing, he usually has the right hand raised with the palm outward, showing he is blessing people. The left hand is extended in a gesture showing that he is giving. In some other statues, he is standing with both hands in front of his chest, palms together. This is the usual Indian gesture that shows both greeting and respect.

When a Buddharupa is sitting down, he is often in the lotus position, meditating. If he is teaching, he is usually sitting with one hand raised. The hand positions are called mudras. Sometimes the first finger of his left hand is pointing to his right hand, and the thumb and first finger of his right hand form a circle. This is called "Setting the Wheel of Law in Motion." It is a reference to his first teaching, when he talked about the wheel of the laws of life. Sometimes his right hand is touching the earth. This refers to the story about the evil spirit Mara tempting him while he was meditating. The story tells that Mara told Buddha his Enlightenment was not real, and that even if it was he would do better to enter nirvana right away rather than remain on Earth to teach others. Buddha's reply was to touch the earth, calling it to witness that there have always been people who have spent their lives trying to help others.

This statue of Buddha at Sukhothai in Thailand shows Buddha meditating. Notice the lotus flowers in the water, another Buddhist symbol.

Pictures and images of Buddha lying down show him at the end of his life, just before he entered Parinirvana. They usually show him as very serene and calm.

Whatever the position, Buddharupas may show any or all of 32 special symbols that show that Buddha was not an ordinary person. For example, there is usually a bump on the top of this head, which is a sign that he had special gifts. He is often shown with a round mark on his forehead, sometimes called a "third eye." No one suggests that Gautama really had this, but it is a symbol that he could see things that ordinary people cannot see. He is usually shown with long earlobes, showing that he came from an important family. His hair is usually curled, a symbol that he was a very holy man.

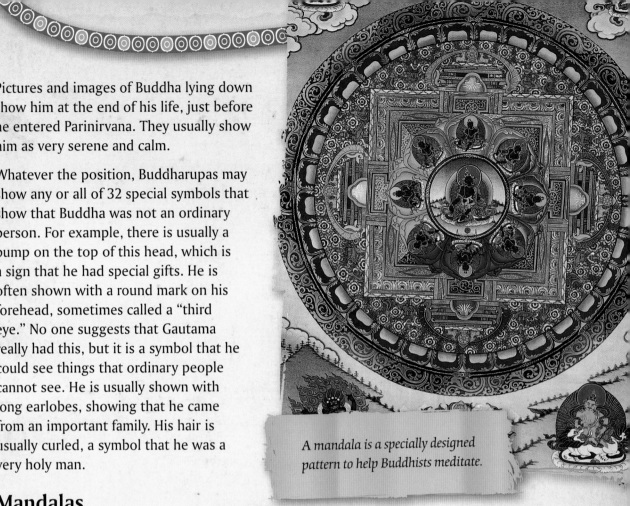

A mandala is a specially designed pattern to help Buddhists meditate.

Mandalas

A mandala is a specially designed pattern made up of circles, squares, and triangles. The Wheel of the Law (the wheel with eight spokes that shows the Noble Eightfold Path) is a mandala. Sometimes they are just patterns, but they may include pictures of Buddha or of bodhisattvas. Some show stages of life and animals. They, too, are symbols—for example, a snake stands for hatred, a cockerel for greed, and a pig for ignorance. Mandalas show Buddhist teachings and are used to help Buddhists meditate.

Lalini's view

Lalini is 15 and lives in Sri Lanka.
Not far from where I live there is a very famous statue of Buddha at a temple called Buddhurajamaha Vihara. My father told me it's 164 feet [50 meters] high. I figured out a long time ago that this means it's 27 times taller then he is! The statue sits at the edge of a park, on a special platform. Buddha is sitting down, meditating in the lotus position. He has his eyes closed and looks very peaceful. His robes are painted bright yellow. I like just going to look at it, to remember what Buddha taught. He looks very kind, and he taught people to be kind to others. I try, but it's hard sometimes!

Ways of Worship

Buddhists may worship on their own or in groups. There is no special day of the week when they meet for worship, but days before the moon is new, full, or at half-moon are important. Many Buddhists believe that Buddha was born, gained Enlightenment, and passed away on days when the moon was full.

Many Buddhists have shrines in their homes.

Shrines

Buddhists usually worship in front of a shrine. A shrine is a special place that is considered to be holy by followers of a religion because of what it contains. Buddhist shrines are beautifully decorated and always contain an image of Buddha, a Buddharupa. Buddhist shrines also contain holders for **incense**, a spice that burns with a strong, sweet smell. There are usually flowers and candles, with places where offerings can be left. Different Buddhist schools have different traditions about other things that may be found in shrines—for example, Zen Buddhist shrines may have offerings of tea, and Tibetan Buddhist shrines have bowls of water in them.

Shrine rooms may also be quite different. In Zen Buddhism the rooms are usually very plain and simple. In other traditions the room may be highly decorated with paintings, candles, and statues. A shrine may be the central point of a monastery or temple, or it may be one room or part of a room in an ordinary house. This is more likely in countries where there are not many Buddhist temples. Some Buddhists, but not all, have shrines in their own homes.

Individual worship

When they worship on their own, Buddhists meditate and chant parts of the holy books. (Chanting is a special sort of singing, using only a few notes.) They often burn incense and offer flowers and sometimes food, such as grains of rice, to a Buddharupa. They may light candles, a symbol of the light of Buddha's teaching. Theravada Buddhists do not pray as part of their worship, but Mahayana Buddhists pray to bodhisattvas for help.

Group worship

When Buddhists meet for worship, it is usually in the shrine room of a temple. Before they go into the shrine room, worshipers remove their shoes. This is to show respect as well as to keep the room clean for worship. There are no seats, so worshipers sit on the floor. Pointing the legs toward the image is disrespectful, so they are kept crossed or pointing to one side. Worshipers may greet a Buddharupa in the shrine by putting their hands together in front of their chest or face and bowing slightly. This is the usual way of greeting anyone in many Eastern countries. Sometimes Buddhists touch their chest, lips, and forehead with their hands to show that their body, speech, and mind are all joining in the greeting. They may bow or kneel and sometimes lie flat on the floor. These are all ways of showing respect to the image.

The people offer gifts of flowers and light (by lighting candles or lamps). In a temple, monks usually carry out the formal parts of the ceremonies. The people watch, meditate, and repeat set words and chants after the monks. There are readings from the Buddhist holy books, and a senior monk often gives a talk. At the end of the ceremony, the people often stay and drink tea together. Tea-drinking ceremonies can be part of worship. The people sit quietly, drinking specially prepared tea from beautiful crockery. There are often flower arrangements. The idea is to be surrounded by peace and beauty.

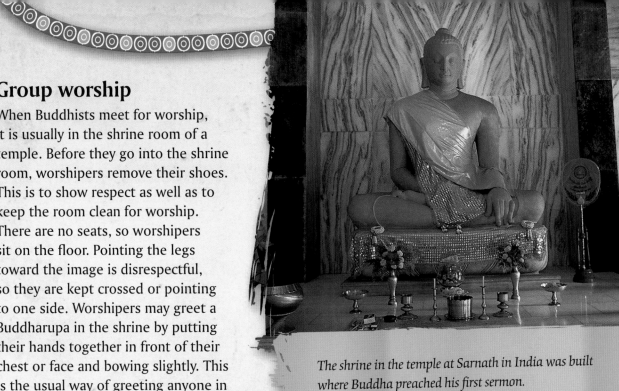

The shrine in the temple at Sarnath in India was built where Buddha preached his first sermon.

Meditation

For many Buddhists, meditiation is the most important part of worship. Meditation is intended to control, develop, and train the mind so that you can go "beyond" thought. The point of meditation is be aware of things without clinging to them or trying to suppress them. Buddhists usually sit on the floor, often with crossed legs, and focus on an object. This may be a Buddharupa or a beautiful object such as a flower. Sometimes they focus on a mantra instead. They try to empty their mind of all other thoughts. Breath is very important in meditation. Buddhists believe that by meditating they will become better people and will be able to achieve Enlightenment.

Buddhist Monks and Nuns

The first order (community) of Buddhist monks was begun by Buddha. At first he would not allow women followers, but he later gave permission for orders of nuns. Today, monks (**bhikkhus**) and nuns (**bhikkhunis**) live in the same way, although the rules they follow are not always exactly the same. There are many more monks than nuns.

Young monks relax in the grounds of their monastery.

Monks live in a monastery, usually called a **vihara**. A vihara is often like a small village. Many are built around a stupa or important temple. The most important room is the shrine room, used for worship and important meetings of the monks. Many Buddhists who live near a vihara go there to worship or study, and children go to school there, to be taught by the monks. In Theravada Buddhist countries, young boys often become monks so that they can be educated in the vihara. They may leave when they become adults. Sometimes Buddhist men become monks for a few months or years to study and learn more about Buddhism. It is not expected that all monks will stay in the vihara all their lives.

Life in the vihara

According to Theravada Buddhist practices, the monks spend most of the day alone, studying and meditating. Buddha taught that helping others is important, so many monks spend part of their day teaching, giving advice to people, or helping in some other way. They eat their main meal before midday, and then fast (go without food or drink) until the following morning— although they may drink water or tea without milk or sugar.

A vihara has small huts or rooms where monks live alone. These are furnished very simply, with a mat as the monk's bed and a small table. The monk is expected to sit on the floor. There may also be a small shrine to help the monk meditate. Anything that is not essential—for example, pens, paper, or books—belongs to the vihara.

The only things that a monk owns himself are the robe he wears—most monks have two—and a few necessary items. These are a needle and thread to repair the robes; a razor, because most monks shave their heads; a bowl and cup for food and drink; and a special strainer to remove any insects from his drinking water. Buddhists try not to kill anything, even by accident.

The five precepts

All Buddhists are expected to follow the five **precepts**, which are the guides for living as a Buddhist. The five precepts are:

◆ not to harm living beings
◆ not to take what is not given
◆ to avoid improper sexual activity
◆ not to take part in improper speech
◆ to avoid alcohol and the misuse of drugs.

When a Buddhist becomes a monk or nun, these rules are followed more strictly. For example, a Buddhist monk should never be alone with a woman. There are also five extra precepts that all monks and nuns, and some other Buddhists, choose to follow. They agree:

◆ not to eat after midday
◆ not to attend music or dancing
◆ not to use perfume or jewelry
◆ not to sleep on a comfortable bed
◆ not to accept gifts of money.

There are also rules of the vihara that monks and nuns must keep.

Alms

Monks are given food and everything else they need by people living around the vihara. This is called giving **alms**. Giving to monks is part of a Buddhist's religious duty, which helps to earn merit. Monks used to go out collecting alms every morning, but today people usually take gifts to the vihara.

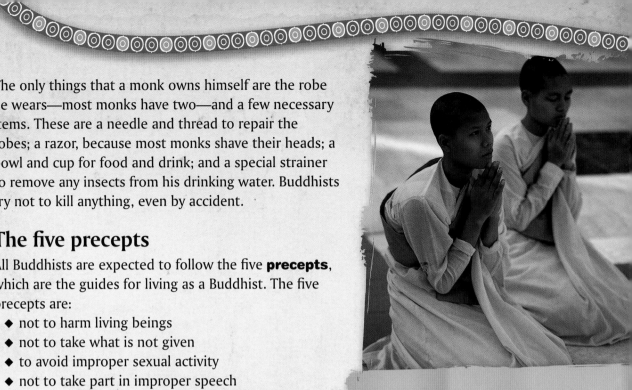

These Buddhist nuns are worshiping at a temple in Myanmar.

Stupas

A stupa is a burial mound or building. The first stupas were built over the places where parts of Buddha's ashes were buried after his body had been cremated. The ashes were divided into eight equal parts and buried in major Indian cities. A stupa was built at the place where the body had been burned, and another where the container that had held the ashes was buried. This gave 10 stupas altogether. Later, other stupas were built to honor the remains of important Buddhists or where other important **relics** were buried. Although their design varies in different countries, stupas are usually built to a symbolic pattern. A mound represents the four elements—air, earth, fire, and water—and a tower or spire represents wisdom.

Buddhist Worship Around the World

You can find the places mentioned in this book on the map on page 44.

The Shwe Dagon pagoda, Rangoon, Myanmar

"Pagoda" is the name for a particular shape of Buddhist temple. The Shwe Dagon pagoda is the oldest Buddhist temple in Myanmar, and one of the most important in the world. Eight hairs from Buddha's head were brought there 2,500 years ago and are still treasured.

The pagoda itself (the pointed section at the center of the temple) stands 325 feet (100 meters) high. The temple was given its present form by King Shinbyusim in 1774, when he covered the pagoda in his own weight in gold. The huge *hti*, or umbrella—the decoration at the highest point of the pagoda that is a symbol of nirvana—includes 1,500

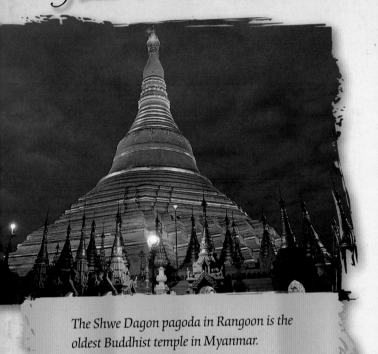

The Shwe Dagon pagoda in Rangoon is the oldest Buddhist temple in Myanmar.

bells, 100 of them gold, the rest silver. The pagoda itself is approached by four covered staircases, one at each main point of the compass. These lead to a marble walkway that surrounds the base of the pagoda. There are places where flowers can be offered, and the whole place is filled with tourists and pilgrims.

The Swayambunath stupa, Kathmandu, Nepal

Swayambunath is built on a hill overlooking the Kathmandu valley. It is reached by climbing 300 steps up from the valley. It has been a center of worship and pilgrimage for 2,500 years and is supposed to have been visited by Emperor Ashoka in the 2nd century BCE.

Swayambunath follows the symbolic pattern of all Buddhist stupas, so the mound represents the four elements. In this stupa the spire consists of 13 rings covered in gold, which represent the 13 degrees of knowledge rising like a ladder to nirvana, represented by the umbrella at the top. Above the umbrella is a golden **vajra** (symbolic thunderbolt), which is a common Buddhist symbol, representing the way Enlightenment comes like a bolt of lightning. On all four sides of the stupa, painted eyes represent the all-seeing eyes of Buddha. The "nose" between them is a Nepalese number one, a symbol of unity. Around the base of the stupa are huge prayer wheels, which are turned by Buddhists as part of their worship.

The Chuang Yen monastery, New York

The Chuang Yen monastery is just outside New York City. It is a center for following the teachings of the Pure Land school of Buddhism. The central part of the monastery is the Hall of Ten Thousand Buddhas, which can seat up to 2,000 people. It contains an image of Buddha that is about 40 feet (11.2 meters) high. This is the largest statue of Buddha in the Western hemisphere. It took eight years to construct and is so large that the hall had to be built around it. Surrounding the building is a terrace that has 10,000 small statues of Buddha as part of a mural. Another important room is the Kuan Yin room. Kuan Yin is an important bodhisattva for Pure Land Buddhists, and the room holds two rare statues of her. One, made of porcelain, is almost 700 years old. The other, made of wood, is almost 7 feet (2 meters) tall and is thought to be over 1,000 years old. The monastery is home to a group of monks and nuns who organize **retreats** for Buddhists, as well as teaching, study camps, and other activities.

The Chuang Yen monastery, near New York City, has the largest statue of Buddha in the Western hemisphere.

Buddhist teaching

This quotation comes from teaching by Phra Ajahan Yantra Amaro, a modern Buddhist teacher. The dharma is Buddha's teaching that all Buddhists try to follow.

Hold a little smile within your heart.
For loving kindness gives the world a peaceful shelter.
Righteousness is dharma.
Oneness of heart is the seat of all nature:
All dharma rises from the oneness of heart.

You can find the places mentioned in this book on the map on page 44.

Pilgrimages

Pilgrimages are journeys that are made for religious reasons. People have many different reasons for going on pilgrimages. For Buddhists, the main reason is that they believe going to holy places, especially places where Buddha lived and worked, will help them in their own search for Enlightenment. They may also visit places such as the stupas where part of Buddha's ashes were buried or famous and important temples. There are 16 sites of pilgrimage for Buddhists, of which four are believed to be the most important. These are the four places that Buddha said his followers should visit.

Pilgrims gather at Bodh Gaya in India, where Buddha gained Enlightenment.

Lumbini

Buddha was born at Lumbini, in what is now southwestern Nepal. The site where he was born is marked by a simple stone pillar that says on it, "Here Buddha was born." This pillar was erected by Emperor Ashoka in 250 BCE and was only rediscovered in 1895. Lumbini is now quite a difficult place to get to, but a small group of monks lives there, and there are temples where people meditate. An ancient shrine marks the very spot where Buddha is said to have been born in a palace garden.

Bodh Gaya

Bodh Gaya is 62 miles (100 kilometers) south of Patna, in India. It is the place where Buddha gained Enlightenment. Buddhists from all over the world visit it, and it is an important meeting place. Many different Buddhist traditions have temples there. On the western side of the temple is a bo tree, said to be descended from the very tree under which Buddha sat to meditate. Close to the tree is a red sandstone slab on which Buddhists believe Buddha sat. Under the tree are carvings of Buddha's footprints, where pilgrims may lay flowers. They may walk around the tree, their heads and feet bare as a sign of respect, and often sit under it to meditate.

The main temple at the site is called the Mahabodhi temple. It has a central tower 160 feet (52 meters) high. Inside is a Buddharupa covered in gold leaf.

Sarnath

Sarnath is the place just north of Varanasi, in India, where Buddha preached his first sermon after he had gained Enlightenment. It was the place where Ashoka erected one of the finest pillars marking a site of importance to Buddhists (see page 9). The capital (top piece) of this pillar has four lion heads and is in the museum there.

Sri Pada, near Kandy, on the island of Sri Lanka, is a very special place for Buddhists because they believe Buddha visited it.

Kushinagara

Buddha passed away at Kushinagara in northern India, and many Buddhists visit the stupa there. The Kushinara Nirvana temple was built in 1956 to make it easier for pilgrims to walk around (circumambulate) the stupa. When visiting a stupa, a Buddhist walks around it at least three times. This recalls the Three Refuges—the dharma, Buddha, and the sangha. Inside the temple is a red stone statue, 20 feet (6 meters) long, of the reclining Buddha, showing him just before he entered Parinirvana. The statue is believed to be 1,500 years old. It was restored in the 19th century.

Other important places

Buddhists may visit many other sites in India and neighboring countries on pilgrimage. For example, on the island of Sri Lanka is a mountain called Sri Pada, the "Sacred Peak." Buddhists believe that Buddha visited Sri Lanka three times and went once to Sri Pada. At the top of the mountain is a stone that has what look like footprints on it. Buddhists believe that these footprints were left by Buddha.

About pilgrimage

According to a 15th-century Tibetan commentary on the Vinaya Sutra, Buddha taught that pilgrimage was very important.

"Bhikkhus, after my passing away, all sons and daughters who are of good family and are faithful should as long as they live, go to the four holy places and remember: here at Lumbini the enlightened one was born; here at Bodh Gaya he attained Enlightenment; here at Sarnath he turned the wheel of dharma; and there at Kushinagar he entered Parinirvana. . . . After my passing away, the new bhikkhus who come and ask of the doctrine should be told of these four places and advised that a pilgrimage to them will help purify their previously accumulated karmas or actions."

Celebrations

Wesak

The Buddhist year follows the cycles of the moon, not the sun. This is called a lunar year. It is shorter than a year that runs by the position of the sun. Buddhist festivals are held on full moon days. The most important is the full moon day in the month of Wesak (also called Vesak), which falls in May or June in the Western calendar. According to Theravada Buddhist teaching, this is the day when Buddha was born, achieved Enlightenment, and passed away. Although the festival has different names in different countries, it is celebrated by Buddhists all over the world.

Buddha Day celebrations are important for Buddhists in many Western countries.

Western countries *(Buddha Day)*

In the United States and other English-speaking countries, the festival of Wesak is often called Buddha Day. Buddhists go to a temple or monastery and listen to a talk by the monks about Buddha's life and his Enlightenment. They often chant and meditate, sometimes for the whole night. Many Buddhists give each other cards and presents to celebrate the festival. The temple is decorated with flowers and streamers, and it is a very joyful occasion.

Sri Lanka

In Sri Lanka, special ceremonies and worship take place in the temples. Streets and temples are lit with huge lanterns with paintings on them showing scenes from Buddha's life.

Sam's view

Sam is 11 and lives with his parents in California.
We always go to the temple on Buddha Day. There are lots of people there, and we all sit on the floor and listen while a monk gives us a talk about Buddha and his teaching. Everyone sits and meditates. I'm still learning how to meditate—it's really hard, because I suddenly find I'm thinking about playing soccer with the kids at school. Then, I have to try to concentrate all over again. It is easier at the temple, because I can sit and look at Buddharupa. He looks calm and peaceful, and I try to remember his teaching. For me, the best part of Buddha Day is the meal at the temple!

People make similar small lanterns to decorate their houses. There are plays and dancing. Part of Wesak is having a good time and enjoying yourself, but the real meaning of the festival is to remember Buddha's teaching. He taught that it is very important to be kind and generous to all living things, so everyone makes a special effort to be kind to others. Many people dress in white clothes and take gifts of flowers to the monasteries. This is to remind everyone what Buddha taught.

Thailand *(Visakha)*

People in Thailand visit temples and monasteries, where monks give talks and preach to people about the life of Buddha. The shrines in the temples are beautifully decorated. A special part of the festival is when the people pour scented water over a Buddharupa, an image of Buddha. At night, the image is taken out of the temple and put on a special platform. People go to the monastery with lighted candles or lamps and carry flowers and incense sticks. They walk around a Buddharupa three times. This is to remember the Three Jewels—once for Buddha, once for the dharma (teaching), and once for the sangha (community). A Buddharupa is therefore surrounded by light and sweet scent.

Hana Matsuri

Mahayana Buddhist countries celebrate the birth of Buddha in April, his Enlightenment in December, and his passing away in February. Hana Matsuri ("Flower festival") takes place in Japan to celebrate the birth of Buddha. It is a spring festival, and people visiting shrines take offerings of spring flowers. People set up stalls and sell food, and there is traditional dancing. Acrobats often perform in the streets. Displays are set up in the grounds of temples to remind people of stories about Buddha's birth. Statues of the infant Buddha are decorated with flowers.

Pouring scented tea over statues of Buddha is a traditional part of the celebrations for Hana Matsuri.

Children may pour scented tea over the statues. This is a reminder of the story that when he was born, two streams of perfumed water appeared from the sky, bathing Gautama and his mother.

Kathina

Kathina is a Theravada Buddhist festival. It is most important in the countries of Sri Lanka, Myanmar, and Thailand. "Kathina" means "difficult" and is a reminder that living as a monk or nun and following Buddha's teaching is not easy.

Every year, Theravada Buddhist monks and nuns have a retreat during the rainy months. This was begun by Buddha himself. They stay in the monastery and concentrate on their beliefs. Kathina takes place at the end of this time— November in the Western calendar. People take a gift of a robe to the monastery. This is to say "thank you" to the monks for the work they do during the year, and it also shows that the people realize how important the monks are.

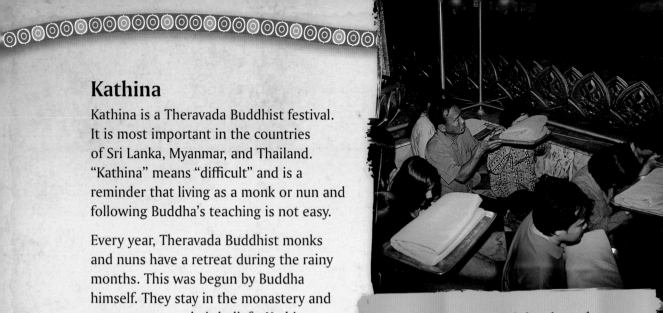

A procession to give cloth for robes to the monastery is part of the Kathina celebrations.

The cloth is usually given to the monastery so that the monks can cut it out and stitch it together in the proper way. The head of the monastery chooses one monk to receive the robe. In Thailand, it is traditional for the royal family to visit monasteries and give robes.

No monk owns things himself, so gifts are always given to the monastery. Giving at this time is thought to earn more merit for the giver.

Songkran

In Thailand, the festival of Songkran takes place in April and lasts for three days. It is the Thai New Year. The day before the festival begins, there is a procession of elephants through towns and villages. Houses and temples are cleaned and dusted, and garbage is removed. This is all part of a fresh beginning for the festival. Everyone eats special foods and wears new clothes. During the festival, Buddhists go to the monastery to give presents to the monks. These are things such as flowers, food, and candles. This is another symbol that the new year is a chance to make a fresh start.

Buddha's teaching about how to live

If a man speaks many holy words but he does not practice their teachings, this thoughtless man cannot enjoy the life of holiness: he is like a cowherd who counts the cows of his master. Whereas if a man speaks but a few holy words, and yet lives the life of those words, free from passion and hate and illusion . . . the life of this man is a life of holiness.
(Dhammapada 1:19–20)

Celebrating Songkran

Water is important in the celebrations of Songkran. (Some people say that this recalls a story about Buddha. The story says that once the king of a country through which Buddha was traveling wanted to keep something to remember him by. Buddha pressed his foot into the sand at the side of a river and left the king his footprint.) Boat races are held on rivers, and there are often water fights in the streets. The festival occurs during the dry season, when it is so hot that smaller rivers dry up. Fish are often trapped in ponds that form as the water evaporates. These fish are rescued by the people and kept until Songkran, when they are released into the deep river. Sometimes caged birds are set free, too. These customs follow Buddha's teaching about how important it is to be kind to all living things. Buddhists believe that by setting the creatures free, they will gain merit.

Like all festivals, the celebrations take many different forms in different places. There is dancing and fireworks. Traditional shadow-plays use a screen with a light behind it, with puppets held so that their shadows fall on the screen. The puppets are attached to sticks with strings so that their arms, legs, and mouths can move. The figures act out traditional stories, with the puppeteers doing the talking. At midnight on the third day of the festival, monks in the monasteries strike a bell and beat a huge drum. The sound builds and dies away three times. After the third time, the festival is over for another year.

Spraying water at the processions is part of the fun of Songkran!

You can find the places mentioned in this book on the map on page 44.

Poson

The festival of Poson is held in Sri Lanka. "Poson" is the name of the month that falls in June/July in the Western calendar. The festival—also called Poson—is held on the day of the full moon. It celebrates the time when Buddhism was first brought to Sri Lanka in 250 BCE. Buddhists believe that in that year the king of Sri Lanka asked Emperor Ashoka to send a missionary so that he could hear for himself the teachings of Buddha. The emperor sent his son, a Buddhist monk named the Venerable Mahinda. He preached to the king, who immediately became a Buddhist. The king then asked the emperor to send an order of Buddhist nuns, and the emperor sent his daughter, the Venerable Sanghamitta. She arrived with a branch of the bo tree in a golden vase. This was planted and it grew. The tree still survives, in the city of Anuradhapura, near the town of Mihintale. The monastery there is called the Shri Maha Bodhi and is named after the tree. "Bodhi" is another name for tree.

Each year, there are processions called **peraheras**, with huge floats. They carry statues that tell the story of Mahinda coming to Sri Lanka. The floats are surrounded by elephants wearing beautifully embroidered coats. Drummers follow the processions, and there are fireworks and dancing. The largest and most impressive processions are at Mihintale, the nearest town to where Mahinda first met the king.

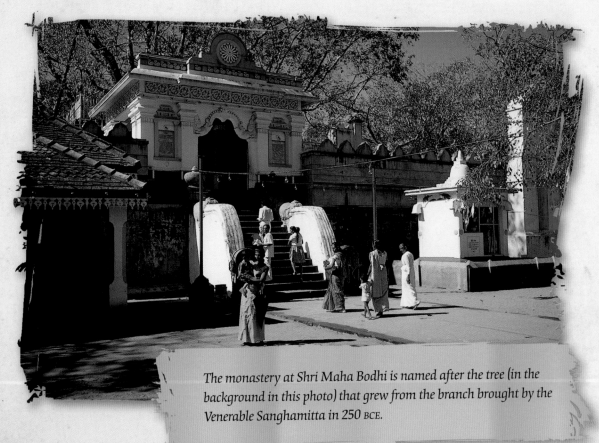

The monastery at Shri Maha Bodhi is named after the tree (in the background in this photo) that grew from the branch brought by the Venerable Sanghamitta in 250 BCE.

Esala Perahera

Esala Day, when Buddhists celebrate Buddha's first sermon, is another important day for Buddhists in Sri Lanka. It is a national holiday, and one of the most impressive celebrations is held in the town of Kandy, in central Sri Lanka. A Buddhist temple there was specially built to keep a relic of Buddha—one of his teeth. This is kept locked away in a special casket (decorated container). For 15 days every August, the festival of Esala Perahera is held in its honor.

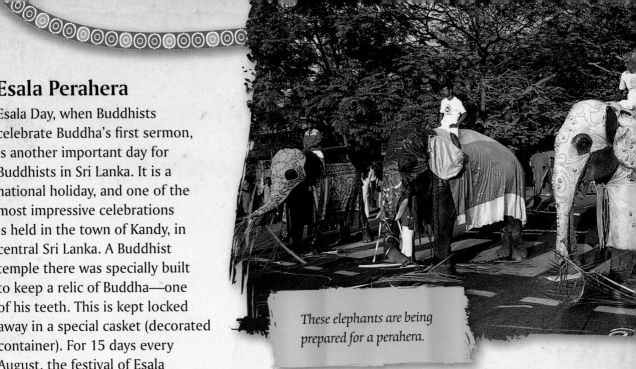

These elephants are being prepared for a perahera.

Buddhists celebrate the bringing of the tooth to Sri Lanka from India hundreds of years ago. The most important part of the festival is the perahera, a procession lit by torches, which takes place on the night of the full moon. Over 100 elephants take part in the procession. They are beautifully decorated and wear brightly colored cloths. The leading elephant carries a casket that is an exact copy of the one that holds Buddha's tooth. (The real one is far too important to be taken out of the temple.) Other elephants carry caskets with relics of other important Buddhists. The procession travels through the town, watched by huge crowds.

Esala Perahera is a religious festival, but it is also a time for enjoying yourself. There is a carnival on the streets. Dancers, drummers, and fire-eaters accompany the procession, and people light fireworks and burn incense and other sweet-smelling perfumes.

Elephants and Buddhist festivals

Many Buddhist festivals use elephants as part of the celebrations. There are obvious reasons for this—Buddhism is at its strongest in countries where elephants have been used for centuries as beasts of burden and for transportation. However, Buddhists also say that it is appropriate that they take part in festival processions because Buddha once used the example of an elephant in his teaching. He pointed out that when a wild elephant is caught, it does not know how to behave and cannot be of any use to its new master. In those days, in order to teach it what to do, elephant trainers would harness a wild elephant to a trusted tame one. The idea was that the tame one could teach the wild one. Buddha advised his followers that they should do something similar in order to learn about Buddhism—they should find a Buddhist whom they trusted, and learn from him or her. Watching elephants in the festivals reminds Buddhists of this teaching.

Losar: A Tibetan Buddhist festival

Mahayana Buddhists celebrate many of the same festivals as Theravada Buddhists, but in different ways. Losar is the New Year festival for Tibetan Buddhists and their most important festival of the year. It begins at the full moon in February and lasts for 15 days. During this time they remember Buddha's early life and the difficulties he had when he first began preaching. Like many other New Year celebrations in different countries, there is a lot of emphasis on a fresh start. As a sign of this, people clean and straighten up homes and temples. There are torch-lit processions led by monks wearing costumes. They wear frightening masks and perform special dances to scare away evil spirits.

Sculptures made from butter are a traditional part of the celebrations at Changa Chopa, the last day of Losar.

The last and most important day of the festival is called Changa Chopa. There are plays about Buddha's life, and monks hold puppet shows. The most spectacular part of the celebration involves sculptures of scenes from Buddha's life. The amazing thing is that the sculptures are made out of butter. They are carved into very intricate patterns and colored with special dyes. There are competitions, and prizes are awarded for the best sculptures.

Japanese New Year

The Japanese use the same calendar as people in Western countries, so New Year is January 1. For Japanese Buddhists, New Year's Eve is more important. This is when the "Evening Bells" ceremony takes place. At midnight, the bells in every Buddhist temple are struck 108 times.

What Buddha said about wisdom

This is the sort of teaching of Buddha that Buddhists think about when they are planning their fresh starts at New Year.

> *If during the whole of his life a fool lives with a wise man, he never knows the path of wisdom, as the spoon never knows the taste of the soup.*
> *But if a man who watches and sees is only a moment with a wise man, he knows the path of wisdom as the tongue knows the taste of the soup.*
> (Dhammapada 5:64-5)

This is a special number for Buddhists, because many of them believe that it is the number of "mortal passions." These include feelings of envy, pride, and jealousy, which spoil people's lives and prevent them from becoming good Buddhists. As the bells ring, Buddhists think about what has been wrong with their lives in the past year, and how they can improve them in the new year.

Obon: A Japanese festival

Obon takes place for four days in July. It is a family festival and, if possible, people go home to their parents to celebrate it. Mahayana Buddhists believe that Buddha can help you in your life, and they pray to him during Obon. They also ask his help for relatives who have died. People visit the graves of relatives. In some areas, spirits of dead relatives are thought to return to the family home, so lamps are lit to show them the way. In other places, there are bonfires. Obon is a serious festival, but it is also celebrated with fairs and dancing. A dance in which everyone joins hands and dances around in a circle gives the festival its name.

Higan: A Japanese festival

Higan takes place at the times of the equinoxes. These are the two times in the year when day and night are of equal length. It is also the time when

This family is taking part in prayers at a shrine in Japan on New Year's Eve.

the seasons begin to change. This reminds Buddhists that they need to change their lives so they can reach Enlightenment. Higan is a time for remembering friends and relatives who have died. Buddhists go to cemeteries to clean and look after the graves and decorate them with flowers. This reminds them that, like flowers, nothing in life is permanent, and their relatives have gone on to a better life. There are special ceremonies that they believe give merit to people who have died. This is important because they believe the extra merit can help the dead on their way to nirvana

Family
Occasions

Buddhists believe there is no such thing as a soul that lives on after death. Buddha taught that the way you live is what is important, and birth and death are just stages on the way to the next life. Therefore, there are very few teachings in Buddhism about the beginning and ending of life. However, for most people, the arrival of a new baby or the death of someone they love is a very important event. Most Buddhists follow the customs of their country. This means that Buddhists in different countries may have quite different customs, because the celebrations are connected to the culture rather than to Buddhism.

In Theravada Buddhist countries, the main ceremonies for a baby happen when he or she is a month old. The baby's head is shaved, because the hair is a symbol of a bad karma (life force) from a previous life. Colored threads that have been blessed are tied around the baby's wrists. Monks are often invited to this ceremony and may be asked to suggest a name for the baby. They prepare a horoscope based on the exact moment of birth. The family always gives food to the monks when a baby is born.

Joining a monastery

Many Buddhist boys join a monastery for at least a few months. This often happens when they are in their teens or their early twenties, but in Myanmar and Thailand almost all boys join when they are 10 or even younger. A boy who joins the monastery at this age is not expected to stay there all his life. Many boys stay for a few years so that they can be educated by the monks.

Boys attend a ceremony for becoming Zen Buddhist monks.

Celebrations in Myanmar

In Myanmar, the ceremony when a boy becomes a monk is called the **Pravrajya ceremony**. The boy acts out the story of how Gautama left his comfortable palace and became a wandering monk. He is dressed like a prince and leads a procession though the streets of his hometown, riding a donkey or pony. When they reach the monastery, he asks the monks if he may be allowed to enter. First, he takes off his prince's clothes, and older monks help him put on the plain orange robe of a Theravada monk. His head and his eyebrows are shaved. (Most Buddhist monks have shaved heads to show that they do not care about their appearance.) The boy promises to obey the Ten Precepts that all Buddhist monks follow, and he is given a new name. This is always from the ancient Pali language, and he uses it for as long as he is a monk. Sometimes a boy's parents give him other presents—a spare robe or the bowl in which he will collect his food.

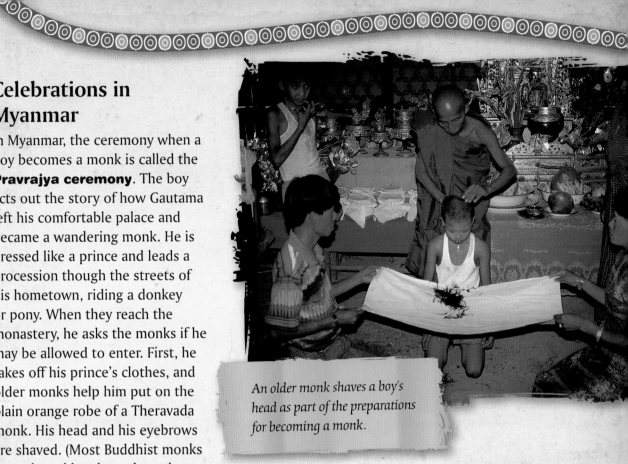

An older monk shaves a boy's head as part of the preparations for becoming a monk.

If a Buddhist girl becomes a nun, she goes through the same ceremony as a boy. However, most girls do not become nuns. In Myanmar, there is a special ceremony for Buddhist girls, which occurs on the day that her brother has his Pravrajya ceremony. The girl is dressed in expensive clothes and has her earlobes pierced with a golden needle. This is believed to be a symbol to show that one day she will marry and wear the fine jewelry that it is traditional for women in Myanmar to wear on their wedding day.

Duties to a son

Buddha said that parents have duties to their son that they must perform. These are to keep him from harm, to show him the right way to live, to teach him, to choose a good wife for him, and to make sure that he has something to inherit. In return, a son is expected to respect his parents and look after them when necessary. He should respect the dead and keep up the honor of his family.

Marriage

Like other family ceremonies, Buddhist marriages may be quite different in different countries, because they mainly reflect the country and the culture in which the couple live. In most Buddhist countries, marriages have traditionally been "arranged"—a young person's parents or older relatives make suggestions about someone who may be a suitable partner. Today, it is becoming more common for a young person to suggest someone he or she knows, and the couple usually meet a few times before the wedding. Both have the right to refuse, but, if they agree to the marriage, astrologers (people who tell the future from the stars) are usually asked to suggest a good date for the wedding to take place.

A traditional Buddhist wedding procession takes place in Hong Kong.

In Buddhist countries, a wedding usually takes place in the bride's home. The ceremony is usually performed by a male relative of the bride, rather than a monk. The couple stand on a special platform called a purowa, which is decorated with white flowers. They usually exchange rings, and the thumbs of their right hands are tied together. Sometimes their right wrists are tied with a silk scarf instead. This is a symbol that they are being joined as husband and wife. Children recite particular parts of the Buddhist holy books, and the couple repeat promises that they will respect and be faithful to each other.

As part of the wedding, a monk may give a talk about Buddha's teaching on marriage. If this does not happen, the couple usually go to the monastery together, before or after the wedding, and listen to Buddha's teaching there. At the end of the ceremony, everyone shares a meal. The celebrations may go on for several days.

Death

Buddhist funerals also reflect the customs of the country in which the person lived. They concentrate on reflecting the person's life and how he or she touched other people's lives. Buddha's teaching emphasized how everything is connected and nothing lasts.

A monk may give a talk about Buddha's teaching, and everyone repeats the Five Precepts and the Three Jewels. In some countries, it is usual for a dead body to be cremated, and the ashes may be collected and placed in a stupa. In other countries, burial is more common.

When people die, their relatives often give gifts to the monks. A common gift is the material for a new robe. They ask that the merit they gain from doing this should be shared with the person who has died. They believe that this may help the person. In Tibetan Buddhism, the Tibetan Book of the Dead is read at the bedside of a dying person and over his or her body. This is intended to help guide the person between the ending of one life and the beginning of the next. This state of existence is usually understood to last 49 days.

At some Buddhist funerals, such as this one in Indonesia, the body is put on a funeral tower for cremation.

MinHan's view

MinHan is 16 and comes from Malaysia.

My grandfather died last year. It was the first time anyone close to me has died. I found the funeral very moving. It was very dignified and solemn, but it was as if everyone there remembered that death really is just a stepping stone to another life. My father and my uncle—his sons—spoke about Grandfather's life and the sort of person he was. My uncle told a couple of stories about him that made us laugh. Then, a monk we know spoke about Buddha's teaching. At the end I still felt sad, and it was strange to know that I will never talk to him again, but I felt sure that everything was right. He had lived a good life, and that was important.

What It Means to Be a Buddhist

As an individual

Buddhists try to follow the teachings of Buddha by following the Eightfold Path, or Middle Way. This tries to avoid extremes, so Buddhists do not choose to live in luxury or in extreme poverty. All Buddhists try to keep the Five Precepts, so they try to live in a way that does not harm any other living being. For example, many Buddhists avoid jobs such as manufacturing guns or weapons, or selling tobacco or alcohol.

A monk in Japan is given food.

How Buddhists live depends on which country in the world they live in. However, Buddhism teaches high standards of behavior, and many Buddhists are pacifists, believing that it is wrong to fight. There are strong traditions of hospitality, and Buddhism teaches that strangers are to be treated with respect and kindness.

Buddha said that family life was important. According to Buddhist teaching, husbands should look after and care for their wives and treat them with consideration and respect. In return, a wife should look after her husband and care for the home and children. Children are expected to respect their parents, which includes previous generations who have died.

Going for Refuge

Buddhists do not actively try to persuade people to become Buddhists but, especially in recent years, many people in Western countries have become interested in Buddhism. They see in it a system of thinking that does not ask them to accept anything that they have not figured out for themselves. Many people feel that they can identify with its teaching about caring for others and the world. The ceremony in which someone becomes a Buddhist is very simple. It is called Going for Refuge. The person states in front of witnesses that he or she wishes to take Buddha as a guide, will follow his teachings, and wishes to become part of the Buddhist community.

In the community

In the days of Buddha, the sangha meant the entire Buddhist community. Today, "sangha" usually refers only to Buddhist monks and nuns. Mahayana Buddhists often use the word to mean a community of followers. Buddhists have a strong sense of community with other Buddhists, no matter where in the world they live. They often refer to other Buddhists as "spiritual friends." Buddha told his followers to join together and help each other, and that this would help them to become more like him.

Buddhism does not have set days for worship, but many ordinary Buddhists go to the monastery or temple on the days of the new moon and the full moon. These days are called Uposatha days. The people take food and other gifts to the monks and join in their meditation. Buddhism teaches that giving gifts to the monks will earn merit for the giver. The idea of giving to others (**dana**) is very important in Buddhism. Buddha taught that the more you give, the less selfish you will become. Buddhist monks do not beg, because it is understood that the gifts they receive are in return for the teaching that is given to the people.

In the world

In the last 20 or 30 years, the ideas that Buddhism has been teaching for centuries have become much more widely accepted. Concern for the environment, and for treating the world as a resource to be cared for, are at the heart of Buddhism. The concern for all living things means that being involved with groups supporting nonviolence is in agreement with Buddhist teaching.

An organic farming site in Ladakh in the Himalayas is an example of Buddhists caring for the environment.

The message of Buddhism

The Dhammapada contains many of Buddha's teachings, including the following:

Our life is shaped by our mind; we become what we think. Suffering follows an evil thought as the wheels of a cart follow the oxen that draw it.

Our life is shaped by our mind; we become what we think. Joy follows a pure thought like a shadow that never leaves.

Map

The globe on the right shows the location of the map below.

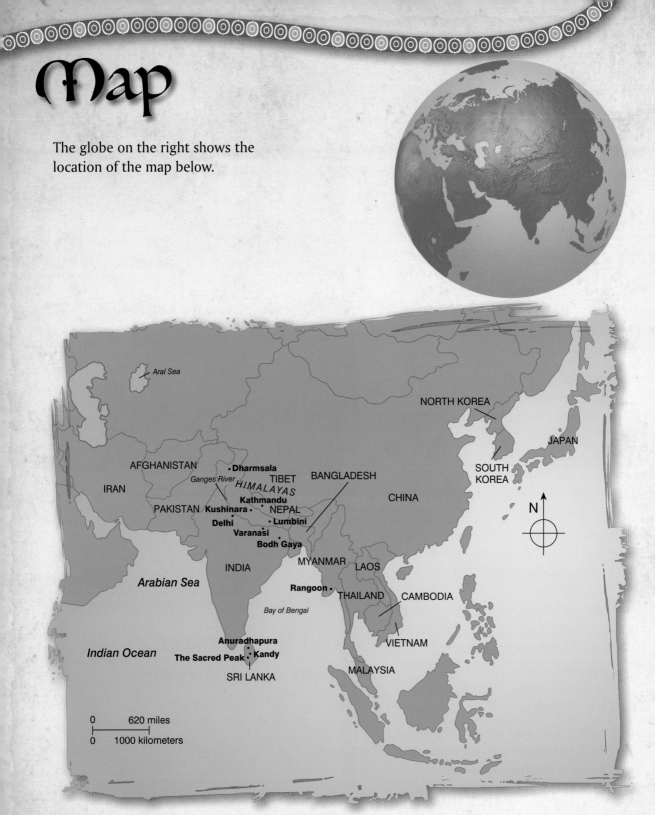

Place names

Some places on this map, or mentioned in the book, have been known by different names:

Kushinara—Kushinagara

Myanmar—Burma

Ganges River—Ganga River

Sri Lanka—Ceylon

Varanasi—Benares

Rangoon—Yangon

Timeline

Major events in world history

BCE	3000–1700	Indus valley civilization flourishes
	2500	Pyramids in Egypt built
	1800	Stonehenge completed
	1220	Rameses II builds the Temple of Amon (Egypt)
	1000	Nubian Empire (countries around the Nile) begins and lasts until c. 350 CE
	776	First Olympic Games
	450s	Greece is a center of art and literature under Pericles
	336–323	Conquests of Alexander the Great
	300	Mayan civilization begins
	200	Great Wall of China begun
	48	Julius Caesar becomes Roman emperor
CE	79	Eruption of Vesuvius destroys Pompeii
	161–180	Golden Age of the Roman Empire under Marcus Aurelius
	330	Byzantine Empire begins
	868	First printed book (China)
	c. 1000	Leif Ericson may have discovered America
	1066	Battle of Hastings; Norman Conquest of Britain
	1300	Ottoman Empire begins (lasts until 1922)
	1325	Aztec Empire begins (lasts until 1521)
	1400	Black Death kills one person in three throughout China, North Africa, and Europe
	1452	Leonardo da Vinci born
	1492	Christopher Columbus sails to America
	1564	William Shakespeare born
	1620	Pilgrims arrive in what is now Massachusetts
	1648	Taj Mahal built
	1768–1771	Captain Cook sails to Australia
	1776	Declaration of Independence
	1859	Charles Darwin publishes *Origin of Species*
	1908	Henry Ford produces the first Model T Ford car
	1914–1918	World War I
	1929	Wall Street Crash and the Great Depression
	1939–1945	World War II
	1946	First computer invented
	1953	Chemical structure of DNA discovered
	1969	First moon landings
	1981	AIDS virus diagnosed
	1984	Scientists discover a hole in the ozone layer
	1989	Berlin Wall is torn down
	1991	Breakup of the former Soviet Union
	1994	Nelson Mandela becomes president of South Africa
	1997	An adult mammal, Dolly the sheep, is cloned for the first time
	2000	Millennium celebrations take place all over the world

Major events in Buddhist history

BCE	c. 563	Siddhartha Gautama (Buddha) born
	c. 528	Buddha achieves Enlightenment
	c. 483	Buddha passes away
	273–232	The reign of Emperor Ashoka of India
	c. 200	Beginnings of Mahayana Buddhism (Madhyamika school)
	c. 100	Holy books written down for the first time
CE	c. 100	Buddhism becomes established in Nepal
	c. 150	First Buddhist monastery established in China
	c. 372	Buddhism is introduced in Korea
	c. 402	Huiyuan founds the Pure Land school
	c. 500	Buddhism becomes established in Korea
		Bodhidharma travels from India to China, bringing Chan Buddhism to China
	538-597	Life of Zhiyi (monk who founded the Tendai school of Buddhism)
	c. 552	Buddhism is introduced in Japan
	629	The Chinese Buddhist pilgrim Xuanzang goes on a pilgrimage to India, where he studies Buddhism and brings back important Scriptures
	c. 600–700	The Chan school of Buddhism in China takes shape
	775	Samye, the first Buddhist monastery in Tibet, is built
	845	Buddhism is repressed in China
	868	Diamond Sutra printed in China (first ever printed book)
	c. 1044–1077	The reign of King Anawrahta (Burma)
	c. 1100–1200	The Rinzai, Soto Zen, and Pure Land schools of Buddhism all develop in Japan
	1222–1282	Nichiren school begun
	c. 1800	Buddhism spreads to the west coast of the United States
	1893	First Buddhist missionary arrives in United Kingdom
	1959	Chinese invade Tibet; Dalai Lama flees to India
	1989	The Dalai Lama is awarded the Nobel Peace Prize

Glossary

alms	giving food and necessities
anatman	Buddhist belief that there is "no soul" or "no self"
anitya	Buddhist belief in impermanence, that nothing lasts
bhikkhu	Buddhist monk
bhikkhuni	Buddhist nun
bo tree	tree under which Buddha was sitting when he gained Enlightenment
bodhisattva	someone who has chosen to be reborn after gaining Enlightenment, so that he or she can help others to achieve it
Buddha	one who has gained Enlightenment (Siddhartha Gautama)
Buddharupa	image of Buddha
canon	approved collection of teaching
cremate	burn a body after death
Dalai Lama	leader of Tibetan Buddhists
dana	generosity, giving to others
Dhammapada	sayings of Buddha
dharma	Buddha's teaching
Diamond Sutra	important Mahayana Buddhist teaching
duhkha	Buddhist belief that everything in the world is "unsatisfactory"
Enlightenment	understanding the truth about the way things are
incense	spice that burns with a strong, sweet smell
karma	life force that a person creates during life
lotus position	position for meditation in which the person sits cross-legged, with the sole of each foot resting on the opposite thigh
Lotus Sutra	important Mahayana Buddhist teaching
Mahayana	school of Buddhism that believes there are different ways to achieve nirvana
mandala	specially designed pattern made up of circles, squares, and triangles
mantra	word or phrase repeated as a prayer and as an aid to meditation
meditation	mental control that leads to concentration and calmness
merit	reward for doing good things
Middle Way	way of life that falls between indulgence and severe self-denial, emphasizing moderation
missionary	someone who travels to tell people about his or her beliefs
monastery	place where monks live
monk	man who has dedicated his life to religion
mudras	symbolic hand gestures
nirvana	end of imperfection

nun	woman who has dedicated her life to religion
Pali	ancient language
Parinirvana	"complete" Nirvana after a Buddha's body has stopped living
perahera	procession that is part of a festival
philosophy	system of thinking
pilgrimage	journey made for religious reasons
Pravrajya ceremony	ceremony in which a boy becomes a monk
precept	guide for living
Pure Land	school of Mahayana Buddhism that teaches that people cannot achieve nirvana on their own
rebirth	Buddhist belief that the five parts of a person re-form to make a new person
reincarnation	belief that after death a soul is reborn
relic	something that is old and treasured (often the remains of a holy person)
retreat	special time for meditation (usually in a monastery)
rupa	statue (of Buddha)
samsara	cycle of birth, death, and "rebecoming" that Buddhists believe in
sangha	community (today, used to describe Buddhist monks and nuns)
Sanskrit	ancient Indian language
shrine	special place of worship
stupa	burial mound erected to house the ashes of Buddha or another important Buddhist
Sukhavati	Pure Land (paradise) in Pure Land Buddhist teaching
sutra	small piece of teaching
temple	name for a Buddhist place of worship
Theravada	school of Buddhism that teaches that each person must achieve Enlightenment on his or her own
Tibetan	from Tibet—school of Buddhism that regards the Dalai Lama as a spiritual leader
Tripitaka	"three baskets"—the most important Buddhist teachings
vajra	symbolic thunderbolt, representing the way Enlightenment comes like a bolt of lightning
Vajrayana	school of Buddhism that emphasizes a close relationship between a leader and followers
Venerable	very respected—a title for Buddhist monks
vihara	Buddhist monastery
Zen	school of Buddhism that teaches that higher understanding will come if people wake up to it

Further Information

Burgan, Michael. *Buddhist Faith in America*. New York: Facts on File, 2003.
Ganeri, Anita. *Buddhism*. New York: New Line, 2006.
Green, Jen. *Japan*. Chicago: Raintree, 2006.
Teece, Geoff. *Buddhism*. North Mankato, Minn.: Smart Apple Media, 2004.

Index